# SERVING BY SAFEGUARDING YOUR CHURCH

## OTHER TITLES IN THE ZONDERVAN PRACTICAL MINISTRY GUIDE SERIES

Serving in Your Church Music Ministry, Randall D. Engle
Serving in the Praying Church, Charles E. Lawless Jr.
Serving as a Church Greeter, Leslie Parrott
Serving as a Church Usher, Leslie Parrott
Serving in the Church Nursery, Julia A. Spohrer
Serving in Church Visitation, Jerry M. Stubblefield

**Paul E. Engle** is an executive editor and associate publisher for editorial development at Zondervan. He has served as a pastor and as an instructor in several seminaries. Among the eight books he has written are *Baker's Wedding Handbook, Baker's Funeral Handbook,* and *God's Answers for Life's Needs.*

**Robert H. Welch** is associate dean at Southwestern Baptist Theological Seminary and an instructor with the National Association of Church Business Administration certification program. He is the author of *The Church Organizational Manual* and a contributor to the *Leadership and Administration* volume in the Leadership Handbook of Practical Theology series.

ONDERVAN
RACTICAL
INISTRY GUIDES

# SERVING BY SAFEGUARDING YOUR CHURCH

PAUL E. ENGLE, SERIES EDITOR
ROBERT H. WELCH

GRAND RAPIDS, MICHIGAN 49530 USA

ZONDERVAN™

*Serving by Safeguarding Your Church*


Requests for information should be addressed to:

Zondervan, *Grand Rapids, Michigan 49530*

Library of Congress Cataloging-in-Publication Data

Welch, Robert H.
Serving by safeguarding your church / Robert H. Welch.
p. cm. — (Zondervan practical ministry guides)
ISBN 0-310-24105-7
1. Church buildings—Security measures. I. Title. II. Series.
BV652.9 .W45 2002
254' .7—dc21

2002007823



*Interior design by Sherri L. Hoffman*

*Printed in the United States of America*

02 03 04 05 06 07 08 /❖ DC/ 10 9 8 7 6 5 4 3 2 1

# CONTENTS

# FOREWORD

## A Lone Gunman in the Church Foyer

On September 15, 1999, something happened that changed my life and the lives of the members of Wedgwood Baptist Church forever. A lone gunman entered the south foyer of the church and opened fire at me and at five of my friends, before proceeding down the hall and into the worship center. When he had finished, seven people were wounded and eight people were dead, including the gunman at his own hands.

That Wednesday night was a little different from most Wednesday nights at Wedgwood. It was "See You at the Pole" day in our community, so our church was sponsoring a post-See You at the Pole rally—an event with several area youth groups participating. The youth were meeting in the main sanctuary, while the adults gathered in the area where the youth usually met on Wednesday nights. The rally included a Christian rock band, skits, speakers, and testimonies about what God had done through the See You at the Pole events that day. While it may seem like a cliché, little did these youth know the testimonies they would have after that evening.

As we sat visiting in the south foyer that evening, we noticed a man about to enter through the glass doors. I didn't recognize the man as being a member of Wedgwood. His presence would not have been unusual, since several adult leaders from other churches were attending the rally already underway in the sanctuary. One thing that did seem unusual, however, was that he was smoking—and he gave no sign that he was going to put out his cigarette before entering the building. Since I was a church staff member, I approached the man to greet him and to inform him that smoking was not allowed in the building. When I was about ten feet from him, he stepped inside the door, pulled a 9mm pistol from under his shirt, and shot me twice, once in the left arm and once in the lower left abdomen.

I immediately went into shock—realizing that I had been shot and that the gunman was now shooting at my friends, but sensing that my body was in a state of suspension. It felt as though my mind had split into two separate impulses. My first thought was to help my friends and to let others know that there was a gunman in the building (and also to call 911); my other thought was that *I* had been shot—and my body and mind did not know how to cope with this situation. I was later told that it is a normal response in these kinds of situations for us to want to help others rather than ourselves.

Later, people would ask me how I managed to stand up after being shot. The fact is, I never fell to the ground. I remember standing for what seemed like several minutes, watching out of the corner of my eye as the shooter fired at my friends and observing their reaction. What seemed like minutes was in reality only a few seconds. For some unknown reason I turned and walked through the glass doors to go outside. I remember still being able to see and hear the gunman and fully expecting him to shoot me in the back, but he didn't. Instead he headed into the auditorium filled with youth.

After I got outside, I examined myself to see how badly I was hurt. I have been asked, "What does it feel like to be shot?" Truthfully, it initially felt as though someone had playfully hit me in the stomach. It really did not hurt, and I did not feel—or even realize—that I had been shot in the arm. I was not bleeding outwardly when I got outside, and I thought maybe I'd been shot with a rubber bullet. Suddenly, though, my stomach pain began to increase rapidly, making me realize that I'd been seriously injured. Shortly after I walked out of the building, my friends came running out—except for one of my best friends, Sydney Browning, whom I found out later was the first person the gunman killed.

Another friend, Larry Clark, who had been in the foyer with us, came out with some others and escorted me into a back hallway of the church and laid me on a bench while they went to assist others. Knowing that I'd been shot, I began to take inventory. I could feel all my body parts, and everything seemed to move. But it really hurt, and it was then that I came to the realization that I could die.

At this point God spoke to me as clearly as I have ever heard him. He spoke simply, softly, and clearly: "You are not going to die." The power in those six words was all it took to sustain me. I believe that God often speaks to us and then allows us to accept his words by faith and act in obedience—and this was one of those times. God's presence and peace completely surrounded me. He did not allow me to decide whether I believed that I would not die; it was true because it was his will. It reminded me of the "Footprints in the Sand" poem; God simply picked me up at that moment—actually even before the gunman entered the church—and carried me. God was not caught off guard by what was happening.

I remember the paramedics working on me and talking about how badly I was hurt, but the thought of dying didn't enter my mind from that point on. Now, what God hadn't told me was that I would spend several weeks in the hospital, undergo several surgeries, and face a long recovery period that extends to this day and will for many days to come. He just promised me that I would not die. I have been told by others, "Now God can really use you because you have a great testimony." I had a testimony of saving grace before, but this just adds to it. Sometimes the most powerful lessons about God are not learned in seminary.

I believe strongly in God's sovereignty. Yet I have mulled over numerous questions as a result of this experience. When people ask why I think God allowed me to stay behind but took Sydney home, I don't have an answer. I just trust that God had a reason. He was not surprised by this shooting. He was in control. I think of the parallels in the story of Job, where the Lord said to Satan, "Have you considered my servant Job?" Satan answered, "Have you not put a hedge around him?" (Job 1:8, 10). I believe that God was in control and that he had put a hedge around me. He allowed events to happen under his control, and it was his decision to take Sydney and leave me. It is not my place to question God, and he doesn't owe me an explanation. When God drew his protection about me and many others that night, he was demonstrating his boundless love, while at the same time letting us know that he was in charge. Sydney and others who died that night died in the love God gave through his Son, Jesus. As the apostle Paul said to the church at Corinth, "Where, O death, is your victory? Where, O death, is your sting?" (1 Corinthians 15:55).

When Bob Welch visited me in the hospital during my recovery, he asked this question: "What do you think you could have done differently?" My immediate response was to say, "Don't ask someone to put out their cigarette!" The truth is that there was very little we could have done in that situation. Our sense of security had been breached. One of the safest places in the world had been violated. In our eyes one of the holiest places—a place where people worship God—was being desecrated. The unheard-of was happening *at church.* I and many others wished that we could have done something to stop it from happening.

At Wedgwood Baptist we've learned that the safest place is still in the presence of God. As we've sought to remove the scars of that night, we have established as our goal to draw closer to God's presence, to place our complete trust in him, and to find our safety in him. While we've made some changes in the way we do things, our church is still an open church to all who want to find Jesus Christ as Savior.

One of Sydney's favorite songs was "I'll Fly Away." Although I have been a Christian since I was eight years old, it was twenty-six years later, on the day of the shooting, that I truly came to know no fear of the sting of death. So I'm ready to fly away to be with God—whenever he calls.

Still in God's Service,
Jeff R. Laster

# INTRODUCTION

Can we expect church buildings to remain safe places in the twenty-first century?

An interesting characteristic of the ancient structures of Europe and the Mediterranean area that have survived from the medieval period is that they appear to have been built for the purpose of fortification and security. In fact, if a menacing army or attacking band of robbers invaded the area, the residents would retreat inside the walls of the fortification and, more often than not, seek sanctuary within the church that existed there. You could find safety from harm within the walls of the church.

As mankind became less barbaric and more civil in behavior, the church took on another role, namely, that of a sanctuary of peace. For centuries the church facility and the individuals who served therein represented the place where God could be found. During periods of famine, pestilence, war, and destruction, it was the church and her parish workers that would bring the community a cup of water and a morsel of bread. These caring folks would bind up the wounds of parishioner and foe alike. Whether the individual was a believer of that particular faith or not, the house of God became a reverenced place to everyone—a place that deserved respect and honor. To defile the house of God was to attack God himself.

When I was a boy in East Tennessee, my Boy Scout troop assumed responsibility to care for a section of the Appalachian Trail that ran through our area. I remember one summer when a group of us hiked our section, cleaning debris and clearing shrubs from the trail. We happened upon a small Primitive Baptist church tucked back in a hollow. It was one of those churches poets write about and artists seek to paint. White siding, a bell tower, arched windows—everything Norman Rockwell was so skilled at rendering. After examining the tombstones in the adjacent cemetery, I concluded that the church had been in existence since the latter part of the nineteenth century. After filling our canteens from the refreshingly cool spring nearby, one guy went over to read the inscription on the door of the church:

ALL WHO ENTER WILL FIND PEACE IN THE PRESENCE OF GOD

Someone turned the handle to the door—and it opened! As we walked into the cool sanctuary, we expected to find a pastor or church member inside. The place was empty except for us. The hallowed quiet was deafening. We lowered our voices and commented on how this church compared to our First Baptist Church in Elizabethton, and then left, closing the door behind us.

Perhaps you can recall a time when your church was open to the public, or perhaps you've heard stories of how—at any time of the day or night—a person could enter the church for prayer and meditation. Sadly, many can only recall the church with locked doors, bars on the ground-floor windows, and security systems. My life has bridged that era of transition. The church where I grew up in the hills of East Tennessee—a church that used to always have unlocked doors—now has locked doors and employs an intercom system by which people can gain entrance. Many churches publicly state that the reason they are abandoning their historic downtown site for a suburban location is that the suburbs are where her members have moved to; yet very likely the unspoken reasons are the hassles of security, the dangers of vandalism, and the concerns for personal safety that exist in the downtown site.

## A NEW DAY IN CHURCH SECURITY NOW EXISTS

In the last century we witnessed an increased level of physical danger to church facilities. Usually the attacks were motivated by some bias or racial meanness. Sometimes the facility was marred or marked by some cultic or devil-worshiping group. And as churches moved into the technology age, thefts occurred of items a thief could quickly sell in an underground market.

It all changed on that Wednesday night, September 15, 1999, when Larry Gene Ashbrook walked into Wedgwood Baptist Church in Texas and asked if this was where those Christians were meeting. Quickly he commenced to shoot indiscriminately in the foyer and then in the sanctuary where the youth were conducting a rally. One of my students, Jeff Laster (the writer of this book's foreword), was the first person shot. Another of my students sat on the couch with the second shooting victim—as her friend died before her eyes. To this day no reason for the shooting has been given—and to this day the hurt continues.

Wedgwood was hardly the first church in which an individual lost his or her life, but it has become a lightning rod around which some have drawn a mark to point to the fact that the church is no longer the respected house of God or the sanctuary of safety for those who come inside her doors. Some would argue that we must return to the fortress mentality that ensured the security of the believer of yesteryear. Others would contend that God is the same God who protects and becomes our comfort and shield in the face of the "enemy."

I am not advocating a fortress mentality in this book. However, I will suggest that it just may be the individuals whom God places in positions of leadership—those who have the responsibility to use their God-given intellect and reason—who will be providentially used to provide the necessary measures to ensure a "house of peace." While God *is* sovereign and *will* prevail, he expects us to use our resources as we shepherd the flock. Even the shepherd described in Psalm 23 was armed with a rod and staff to ward off danger and to shield from the attack of wild animals. When the sheep were brought into the fold in the evening, the shepherd became the "door" at the entranceway, sleeping at the opening in order to keep the sheep from harm. As the pastoral psalm states, "Even though I walk through the valley of the shadow of death, I will fear no evil, for you are with me; your rod and your staff, they comfort me."

This shepherd analogy is important for all church leaders to keep in mind. Most of us are fulfilled when we are able to feed the flock and lead them into pleasant pastures of existence. We often fail to recognize that shepherding a flock requires us to become administrators and functionaries. This small book will assist you in that part of your ministry, whether you are an ordained staff member or a lay board member. My hope is that this material will be of general use to you and of particular use to the individuals or groups you designate to implement facets of practical security in your church. Your church might find it helpful to give a copy of this book to a select group of leaders to read, to discuss, and then to develop a practical action plan.

# ONE

## Building for Security

One of my many jobs in my twenty-two years in the Navy was that of an "inspector general" of an engineering component of the Department of Defense. My duties included evaluating the project that was designed by the Navy and completed by a contractor. Early in this tour, I became deeply concerned about the wide variance between the cost that was estimated for a job and the actual money given to a contractor at the completion of the job. I discovered that the vast difference was due in part to the poor design by my organization's engineers. Bidding contractors would look at the blueprints and specifications and find the numerous flaws and then bid low, knowing that after they were awarded the contract, they could get change orders written. Their profit was not in the contract but in the numerous costly change orders granted.

Now my momma didn't raise a dummy. That was my daddy's and my own tax dollars that were being wasted! I told the engineers that they had to create excellent working documents and that the contract would be built exactly as they designed it—with no change orders granted. What's more, I told them that if errors existed after the project was completed, they would have to go in after the fact and fix it themselves. It took a few poorly designed jobs for them to realize that I was for real. In time the Navy started getting its money's worth on contracts.

## PLAN AHEAD FOR SECURITY

I learned an important lesson in this experience: *The design is important.* And, most important of all, it costs a whole lot more to go back in and fix something after the fact than to do it right in the first place. As a member of a church, I have served on three building committees, and as a professor of administration, I have consulted with numerous other churches about their building program. Guess what issue is not on the top of their list of concerns for the building program (actually, most of the time it doesn't even make the list): SECURITY. Everybody has their own agenda: The deacons and elders want to know how we're going to pay for it; the pastor wants to know if it will look good; the parishioner wants to know if the seats will be comfortable; and on and on it goes. Even the media personnel are typically not concerned with the security of their expensive equipment, just with the need for it to look good and to sound good. Before I discuss issues relating to good building techniques with security in mind, I want to deal with the important issue of planning.

## ASSIGN A WORK GROUP TO STUDY SECURITY ISSUES

Even though this book's main focus is not on planning for and erecting a church building, the topic must be briefly introduced. Most building programs begin with a perceived need, then a study group is formed to visualize the perception, and finally a building committee is created to plan for the building project—whether new construction or remodeling. To ensure that the project glorifies God and not human beings, I would strongly suggest that individuals who serve on these groups be church leaders (including the pastor) who have a vision for the church and community and who are spiritually attuned to the church's mission. Let's give the name "Project Steering Committee" to this latter group. We'll use the term *steering* to indicate that this group controls all facets of the project from design to construction to paying for it.

Each member of the steering committee will be assigned leadership in the development of several subcommittees that will see the project details through. One subcommittee may be assigned the role of acquiring land, another the role of overseeing a finance campaign, while still another the role of generating publicity for the project. A subcommittee will be formed to work with the architect in the design of the facility, possibly another subcommittee to work with the builder, and maybe even another to select the furnishings for the new facility.

It is at the subcommittee level that work groups need to be formed. The steering committee provides general and *spiritual* leadership. The subcommittees provide general and *practical* expertise. The work groups become subelements that research and recommend *specific details* for the project. For example, in the design of a sanctuary, who best to recommend media requirements to the design subcommittee than a work group composed of individuals who are familiar with the equipment, who will operate it, and who will have to answer to Aunt Maude when she complains that the music is too loud.

Note the following chart of how the Design and Construction subcommittee might use work groups for a sanctuary remodeling project:

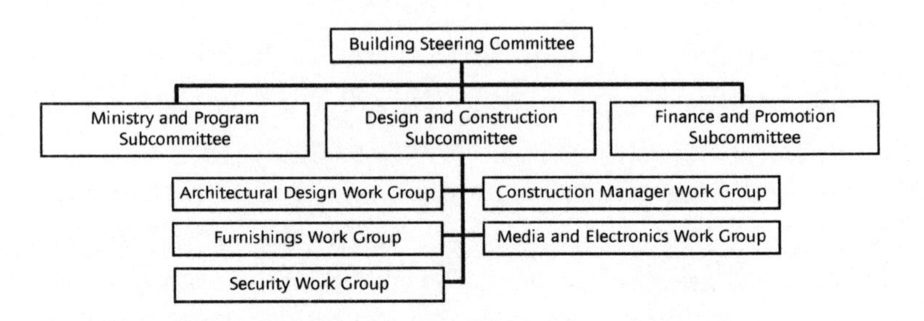


I strongly recommend the formation of a work group of persons who are familiar with security systems and resources that aid in the design of secure facilities, as well as those persons who have practical knowledge in security measures. This group becomes the research foci for dialogue with community and law enforcement agencies that have offices that can help in the practical aspects of the design. These work group members go online to the hundreds of sites that describe security systems

---

A word of advice about searching for Web sites relating to security. As I was writing this book, I went to a popular Internet search engine and asked for information about "security." The response was over 1,885 sites that mention security! I went back and asked for "security systems" and got 1,217 sites that discussed this topic. When I asked the search engine to locate sites that talked about "building security," I was given 73 sites. When I narrowed the search even further to "building security systems," I got a manageable 32 sites to explore. When I went to these sites, I found several duplications. So in the end I was able to review information from approximately 16 organizations that provided building security systems that would apply to churches. The Internet is a wonderful research tool, but it can be overwhelming unless used wisely.

---

and measures. They observe and evaluate existing systems and talk with the people who operate them.

"Wait a minute! Isn't the architect supposed to do this?" you ask. Well, yes and no. Architects are gifted men and women who want to please their clients and receive their just reward. They listen to their clients and provide them with what they want in a buildable, well-engineered, safe structure. Yet I've discovered that, while they are by and large very talented and competent designers who are familiar with the latest construction techniques and materials, most are not security technicians. If you want security as part of the package, they are usually happy to hire a consultant for you and charge you accordingly. Or you can form a work group and tell them what you want—and maybe save a buck or two in the end.

## CONSIDERATIONS FOR DESIGNED SECURITY

Remember the story of the three little pigs? The pigs who built their church—I mean, their house—of straw and wood had the house blown down by the big bad wolf. It was the smart pig—the one who used bricks—who built an enduring structure. I think Scripture has a word or two to the wise. We are admonished to avoid building with wood, hay, or straw (1 Corinthians 3:10–15) and seek instead to build with durable materials. Jesus even talked about building on a firm foundation where our structure will not be washed away (Matthew 7:24–27). The choice of your building or remodeling materials will determine to a large extent the level of your interest in safety and security. Here are some considerations that your security work group can evaluate:

## Build Exterior Walls with the Most Durable Material

Stone, brick, or masonry are obvious first choices. The more durably the structure is built, the more secure it will be. Think of the long-term maintenance of the structure. While it may be cheaper to build a wood-sided building, be sure to evaluate the costs throughout the lifetime of the structure. It is probably more cost-effective to construct a more durable and secure exterior.

## Provide Secure Entry Points

Law-enforcement officials report that nearly 90 percent of those who violate property gain entrance through the desig-

---

I need to make something clear early in the book: No structure, however durably it is built, is totally impenetrable. In recent years, movies, television shows, books, and other media have idealized the ingenious individual who penetrates the most secure system designed by humanity. Given enough time and resources, any structure can be entered. The objective of most security measures is to discourage or hinder access, not prevent it. The vast majority of the items discussed in this book will address the issue of discouraging and hindering access or penetration into the facility. The more we do—and the better we do these things—the better our security system will be. When you lock a door, install a TV camera, have an adult remain with your children, or provide a roving patrol of your parking lot, your objective is to create the mind-set in the potential perpetrator, "It's too hard; let's move on to where people haven't done anything to make their place secure."

---

nated entry points of the facility—the doors and windows. For example, Larry Gene Ashbrook walked in the front door of Wedgwood Baptist Church!

*Doors*

- ❑ Specify metal-clad or solid-core doors on all exterior doors.
- ❑ If doors have a window, use a more secure pane, such as
  - ❖ wire glass—two pieces of glass, fused together, with a wire mesh molded in between.
  - ❖ tempered glass (often called safety glass)—a thick glass that will shatter when hit extremely hard but will withstand most attempts to break it.
  - ❖ laminated glass—two glass panes with a thin sheet of plastic fused between (this is often called automotive glass or hurricane/storm glass); even if it breaks, it won't allow entry.
  - ❖ plastic laminates—Plexiglas, an acrylic product that will break but not shatter, and Lexan, a polycarbonate that is practically indestructible; these are often used to protect art/stained glass.
- ❑ Use molded hinges—a hinge that restricts the removal of the hinge pin.
- ❑ Use dead bolt-type locking devices on doors that do not have panic hardware installed.
  - ❖ On doors that lead to the exterior that are located there because of fire code requirements for multiple exit doors, use surface-mounted, vertical dead-bolt systems that are thumb-latch operated only or key entry from the *exterior* only. Remember, such doors are

there for safety and for emergency exit and must be able to be unlocked from the inside without a key—they *don't* have to be opened from the outside.

- ❖ Dead bolts should have a minimum of twelve-inch throw and penetrate a solid frame—either wood or metal. Do not install an interior-keyed dead bolt on an emergency exit; these systems must have an interior thumb latch.

- ❑ Install magnetic/electronic sensors on doors—especially doors that have emergency panic hardware.

*Windows*

- ❑ Specify metal or metal-clad windows on all ground-level windows.
- ❑ Use windows that are made up of several smaller panes of glass held in place by mullions affixed to the window frame. This creates a security grid.
- ❑ Thermo-pane windows not only provide energy efficiency but also offer a thicker window glass for security.
- ❑ Ground-level windows must have a locking device that immobilizes any moving window element. Additional window-locking systems will be discussed in chapter 4.
- ❑ Windows to crawl spaces, equipment or mechanical rooms, storage spaces, and other unoccupied areas may have fixed securing systems—bars or pin locks, or even sealed shut—as long as the primary emergency exit is through the entry door.
- ❑ Fire safety codes will require ground-level access to spaces occupied by children up to age eight. Windows or doors

from these spaces should have magnetic or electronic sensors installed to monitor their security condition.

### *Entry Lights*

- ❑ All primary entry points (doors where people go in and out) should be well lit.
- ❑ Provide two light fixtures in case one burns out.
- ❑ Lights should be on either from dusk to dawn or come on when someone approaches the door.
- ❑ Low-voltage metal halide or fluorescent systems provide the most economical source of light.
- ❑ If the entry point opens into a foyer, then the foyer should be also illuminated during the same period as the exterior lighting.

### *Sensor Systems*

- ❑ Most magnetic or electronic sensing mechanisms require a wire to the element. It is significantly more cost-effective to install this system at the same time the doors and windows are installed because the wire will have to be placed inside the door/window jamb for both aesthetics and security. Make sure that sensors on ground-level doors and windows are inside the door or window unit rather than mounted outside. Two practical reasons: First, if a sensor is hidden in the entry unit and the jamb, the intruder does not know where it is and therefore will have difficulty placing a magnetic override. Second, it just looks better.

- ❑ Install break-sensitive tape or a noise sensor when large areas of plate glass are on the ground level.
- ❑ Whether or not a security system is actually installed at the time of the building construction, provide a metal conduit to every entry point to enclose the wiring for the system. This will facilitate later modifications or additions. Do not mark the conduit and boxes as security system sources. Blueprints should have the system marked, but do not point a finger to your system for a burglar to override or jam.
- ❑ Centralize the monitor and source of security systems in an office or another secure location. If required, provide alternative power and secondary phone connections.

## Design with a View in Mind

Both Peter (2 Peter 3:10) and Paul (1 Thessalonians 5:2) would describe Jesus' return as an occurrence similar to "a thief in the night." They were probably reflecting on Jesus' teaching about preparedness as Dr. Luke recorded it in Luke 12:39: "But understand this: If the owner of the house had known at what hour the thief was coming, he would not have let his house be broken into." Jesus' dialogue with Nicodemus reveals that evil people love darkness: "Everyone who does evil hates the light, and will not come into the light for fear that his deeds will be exposed" (John 3:20).

Nearly seventy times in Scripture darkness is associated with evil. Generally, human beings do not like to have their wickedness in full view. As you plan a building program, consider the facility from the eyes of the thief, the child molester, the rogue who would deface the property:

- ❑ Are entry points (windows and doors) hidden from view, or are they fully exposed? Doors should be adjacent to parking areas or street entries. Windows provide illumination and ventilation. If this is not necessary in a particular space, consider eliminating windows or reshaping them to a smaller opening.
- ❑ Are windows bigger than they need to be? Instead of having one large window in a space, consider two or more narrow windows that make movement through them difficult. If light is the objective, consider placing windows in a horizontal position near the ceiling of the room.
- ❑ Build in exterior wall illumination with low voltage down-lighting in the soffits.
- ❑ Provide elevated lighting in parking areas (more will be said about parking lot lighting in chapter 3). Even if the budget does not allow for the lighting now, run the conduit to where the lights would be, in order to prevent tearing up a parking lot later on.
- ❑ Landscape with low, slow-growing shrubbery around the building. Plant your trees and taller shrubs in medians some distance away from the building.
- ❑ Consider locating playgrounds away from the view of a passerby but in full view of those who are responsible for monitoring the safety of the child. Many churches will place a fence or shrubbery line between the roadway and the play area.

## QUESTIONS FOR REFLECTION AND DISCUSSION

In this chapter we've seen that physical security begins with the plan for the facility. Whether or not you will have an opportunity to build or to remodel your facility, it is important to think about the things that should be (or should have been) integrated in the design of the facility. With this checklist in mind, you can set about to correct and improve the security of your facility:

1. Do you know where the plans to your facility are stored? Who was the architect? Are these plans up-to-date?

2. If it were necessary to build a new facility or remodel your existing facility, who in your church are the mission-conscious individuals you would want to serve on the project steering committee in order to ensure that the church's purposes are fulfilled?

3. Given some of the above suggestions for incorporating security into the building process, create a checklist to use in inspecting your church to determine its potential for providing a secure facility.

4. Whom would you ask to assist you in inspecting the church?

# TWO

# Organizing for Security

Security doesn't just happen. It takes planning, money, and people to make it work. In chapter 1 I considered security as one crucial feature of a building or remodeling process. I explored some things that a church and her leadership could consider to "build in" security at the outset. My rationale was this: It's easier and better to provide a secure space up front than to have to retrofit the facility in order to accomplish a safe and secure environment.

This same philosophy carries over into this chapter: It is better to proactively put in place procedures that will ensure that the individuals who utilize the facility are doing so in a safe and secure manner. Because churches are people-product organizations, her leaders must address the human resource factors in providing a secure facility.

You've probably heard the human resource axiom, "It is far easier not to hire a problem employee than to have to deal with that problem employee later." For our purposes the phrase might be altered to state that it is far easier to employ individuals who pose no security risk than to deal with security issues after these individuals are part of the organization.

This chapter will deal with two principal issues: (1) How you establish an organization that will deal with the issues of security, and (2) How you select individuals who will contribute to a safe and secure facility.

## DO YOU NEED A SECURITY COMMITTEE?

You may not want to hear the answer to this question, but here it goes: "It depends." "That's not helpful!" you shout, and you are right. So, because I want this to be a helpful book, let me explain the answer, and then you can decide for yourself what type of organizational structure you need for your particular church.

I am a member of a Baptist church. Now Baptists are notorious for forming committees. If you are a member of another denomination, or perhaps involved in an independent church, the chances are that your church has at least some committees. Historically, the democratic polity of churches in my tradition demands that we have a committee for nearly every function a church or church-based organization could carry out. In recent years, however, some of us who have studied organizational dynamics have urged a modification of this mind-set.

## BOARDS, COMMITTEES, COUNCILS, AND MINISTRY TEAMS

In the local church a variety of groups exist to provide direction and to function as the leadership in the doing of ministry. Conceptually these can be categorized as either providing *polity* (developing policy and giving guidance) or *activity* (carrying out the functions of ministry).

### Policy-Making Groups

Every church will have a polity body. These will often be called boards or committees, and they have one principal function: to provide the rules and regulations of the organization. These polity bodies exist in groups like denominational/diocese/presbytery boards, boards of elders or deacons, pastors and pastoral staff, and a host of committees. Polity bodies have certain characteristics:

- ❏ They are designated in the organization's constitution and bylaws.
- ❏ They have an elected or selected membership.
- ❏ Their terms of office are usually defined in the constituting documents.
- ❏ The constituting documents state that this group has the authority to act on behalf of the corporate body.
- ❏ Such boards and committees are duly recognized by authorities (both secular and ecclesiastical) as representing the consensus of the institution.
- ❏ They define, develop, or delineate the rules by which the church or organization will function. In some instances, especially in the democratic polity forms of church government, the board or committee will report actions or decisions to the institution for their approval.

In chapter 1 I discussed the creation of a building or project steering committee. The function of this committee is to act on behalf of the church body in matters of land acquisition; contractual agreements with consultants, architects, and contractors; entering into loan agreements with banks or lending agencies; and other similar matters. In other words, these committee members are given the authority to act for the church.

Every church should have groups formed to make polity decisions in four principal areas:

1. ecclesiastical and theological context
2. personnel
3. financial operations
4. facility (building) management

A board will usually be assigned the responsibility for the first; committees will typically be established for the other three areas. With regard to security issues, all four polity groups will come into play:

- ❑ The board will be responsible for establishing the statement of relationship between the church's mission and the community in which the church carries out her ministry.
- ❑ The personnel committee will be responsible for defining the character of the church's leaders and then defining the expertise of paid and unpaid church workers.
- ❑ The finance committee will be responsible for calculating the monetary expenditures necessary for maintaining a safe and secure work and worship environment and for establishing rules for the secure handling of church funds.
- ❑ The facility committee will be responsible for providing a safe and secure work, study, and worship environment.

## Worker Bees

If the three committees are responsible for *making policy* in the areas of personnel, finance, and facility, who actually gets the work done? This is where councils and ministry teams come into play. In chapter 1 I observed that the steering committee had several subcommittees that went out and researched and did the work on behalf of the committee. This is the role of the councils and ministry teams.

A *council* is an advisory group. The wisdom of Solomon is so apropos here: "Plans fail for lack of counsel, but with many advisers they succeed" (Proverbs 15:22). More often than not, councils give advice to a staff minister. For instance, the pastor may have a church council, made up of the various program leaders, that provides advice, information, coordination, and evaluation of how the church is going. They become the pastor's eyes and ears, as well as the emissaries of program decisions that are made. Various councils could be established to assist staff ministers in different areas: preschool or children, youth, adults, singles, recreation, and so forth. A person serves as a council member usually because of some position he or she holds or as a result of being selected by his or her peers.

A *ministry team* is a group of members who come together out of a desire for service based on a perceived spiritual gift or some skill or interest they possess. These are not policy-making groups. They usually act within the bounds of a fixed budget allocation and under the guidance of a staff member or polity group. While recognized by the church, they are not usually "elected" members. The parking lot greeter ministry team is an example of a ministry team (I'll talk a bit more about this team later on in the book). The folks voluntarily stand outside in all kinds of weather, directing visitors to the church entrances, assisting in parking, and performing such security functions as patrolling the parking lot. Several existing ministry teams may well be helpful in enhancing your church's security functions (such as ushers, child-care workers, money counters, media specialists, and maintenance volunteers). Your church may even choose to form a security ministry team specifically commissioned to coordinate and carry out the security functions of the church.

## CREATING ORGANIZATIONAL STRUCTURE

Now that we have a conceptual understanding of a way to organize for doing the work of the church, let's look at some practical suggestions for organizing *for security.* I want to consider this topic in two venues: (1) How do we create an organization for security? and (2) What are the personnel issues we should be aware of as we develop a secure environment for our parishioners?

### The Organization

There is a risk that you will close this book soon, convinced that the example below won't work for your church. But I urge you to bear with me and remain open to the possibility that at least some elements will work in your particular context.

---

Since this is a series of practical ministry guides for church leaders, I'll assume that you are either the pastor or an associate designated by the pastor to develop a system of security for the church. Or you may be a lay member who serves as a trustee. Much of what is said in the next few pages will be addressed to those who serve as administrators in the church—those given the responsibility to put this security program in place. I'm presenting the broadest concept of this subject; you may pick and choose the elements you wish for your particular application.

---

Let's consider a hypothetical situation:

- ❑ A governing *board* exists—I'll call this board the board of elders.
- ❑ A ministerial *staff* exists, appointed by the board, for the purpose of carrying out the mission and functions of the church—I'll call them the pastor and staff members.
- ❑ *Committees* exist that develop policy for the church.
  - ❖ The *personnel committee* selects all ministerial and support staff.
  - ❖ The *finance committee* coordinates the finances of the ministries of the church
  - ❖ The *facility committee* is responsible for a secure work, study, and worship environment.

The board will define the character of the church's ministry. It will make broad policy statements such as "our church is to be open to everyone" or, "out of concern for the safety of our employees, only certain designated doors and spaces will be open." It will establish ministries such as a weekday early education school, a twenty-four-hour prayer ministry, and benevolence or community assistance programs that will fit well with the board's perception of the spiritual nature of its church's ministry—and that will require security considerations.

The ministerial staff, under the leadership of the senior pastor, will develop, implement, coordinate, allocate, and administer the mission direction of the board. (If your ministerial staff is a party of one, namely, you, then you may want to form a council that can help you administer the programs and ministries of the church. Your objective is to delegate the work so that you can free yourself up to carry out the important task of *leading* the work!) Assign a ministerial staff member to work with each of the polity committees. Senior pastors should ask the staff member to be the liaison between the board and the committee that is accomplishing the job through direct action and through the formation of ministry teams.

---

In Scripture we find three basic types of organizational structure:

**The One-Man Show**

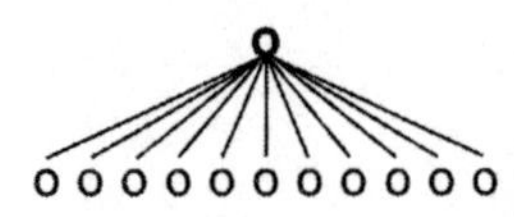

In this type of organization everyone reports to the boss. This is the problem Jethro saw with regard to Moses in Exodus 18, where Jethro warned Moses that he would burn himself out trying to do all the work himself.

**No One Is in Charge**

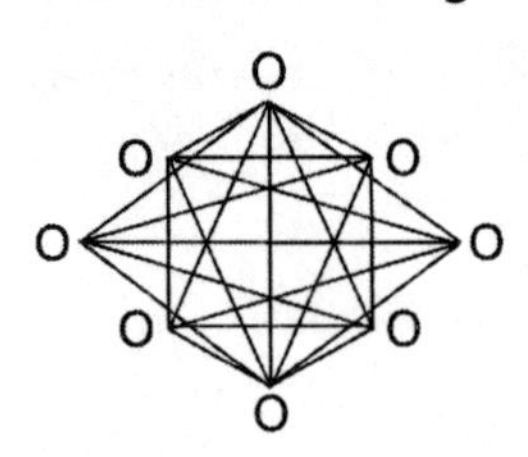

In this type of organization there is no leader. This is sometimes called a *collegial structure* in which everyone is equal. In 1 Corinthians 14:40 this type of structure is rejected by Paul as being confusing, and he notes that God's work is to be orderly and is to be appropriately accomplished.

**Delegated**

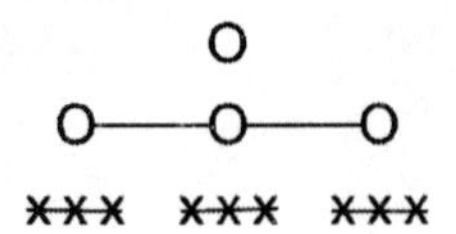

In this type of organization there is a leader. This is what Jethro suggested to Moses: Place leaders in charge of thousands, hundreds, and so forth. Jethro told Moses to delegate the lesser tasks and concentrate on the important issues only Moses could accomplish. Looking at how the apostles are listed in Scripture, they seem to be organized in three groups under Peter, Philip, and James son of Alphaeus (see Matthew 10:2–4; Mark 3:16–19; Luke 6:14–16; and Acts 1:13).

A discouraging word for readers who are pastors. Know this: If the roof leaks, it's *your* fault! You may have in place an assigned administrator who works through a facility committee that has a building and grounds maintenance team—and you have delegated to these groups the responsibility of keeping the roof from leaking. But in the parishioners' eyes, it is still your fault, because you are "in charge." But that's okay, because you *do* have in place an organization that can get the roof fixed. In fact, as Jethro told Moses, you only have to deal with one person—the administrator—who will work with the committee, who will authorize the working ministry team, and the roof gets fixed. "Too many thumbs in the pie," you say? Well, maybe so. But it sure beats *your* having to find someone to fix the roof. The pastor can hold the administrator accountable, who in turn holds the committee accountable, who in turn holds the ministry team accountable for repairing the roof.

The same philosophy can be tapped into for creating an organization to ensure security in the church. In the small church that doesn't have a ministerial staff to support the pastor, the chairpersons of the various committees become the advisers who work directly with the pastor to receive delegated responsibilities. They in turn work in their committees and form ministry teams to get the job done. In a small church, for example, the pastor delegates to the facility committee chairperson the responsibility to lead the committee in developing policies for providing a safe and secure structure. To the finance committee chairperson is delegated the responsibility of leadership in setting aside fund allocations to pay for the security initiatives and to form policies for accounting and for auditing funds. And to the personnel committee chairperson will be delegated the responsibility to research and develop policies that will ensure that church personnel who work there are the kind of people who will not violate the security and safety of church members.

Each of these committees may recommend the formation of a variety of ministry teams. For example, the personnel committee may suggest a preschool/children/youth worker screening group to implement a policy stating that any adult who works in (or is in the proximity of) ministry to children up to the age of eighteen must have a background investigation. Or they may form a subcommittee ministry team to evaluate all applications for paid worker positions in response to a policy

---

What about pastors of small churches or beginning churches? Do they form a group of committees to assist in the administration of the church? Because almost half of the churches in America fall into this category, let me comment briefly. Your basic need is to *involve as many persons as possible in the life of the church.* Committees, councils, and ministry teams are effective ways to do this. Your objective is to delegate the workload to trusted and trained parishioners, and, more important than that, you want them to have ownership of the church program! *Every church needs polity organizations.* For some small churches I recommend that they consider combining the functions of personnel and finance into one committee—an administration committee. Another committee, called the physical resource committee, can be assigned all the property subfunctions. As the church matures and grows, ministry teams can develop out of these two committees.

---

requiring the use of an application form that inquires about an applicant's character, background, and ability.

The finance committee may have subgroups assigned to count money each Sunday and provide security for the bank-depositing task. Annual audit teams may be formed to review the policies for handling money and to evaluate whether funds received have been appropriately accounted for. The committee may appoint a special stewardship team to coordinate a unique fund-raising event.

The facility committee may form an emergency response team (the ERT will be discussed more fully in chapter 3) that will be prepared to respond to critical situations that may take place at church. Or the committee may delegate to an usher team the responsibility of perimeter or building security during worship services. A ministry team may be formed of individuals who roam the church grounds and hallways during services to provide security.

Remember the story in Acts 6 where a problem arose in the early church? The widows of Grecian Jews were not being taken care of in the same manner as the widows of Hebraic Jews. The leaders (the apostles) declared that it wasn't their primary responsibility to minister ("wait on tables") to the widows. They instructed the church to form a ministry team to carry out this ministry. The leaders gave instructions concerning the character and capability of the persons to be selected. After these persons were chosen, the church brought the names to the apostles, who then delegated to them this particular responsibility. While some point to this passage as the appointment of the first deacons, I like to call it the establishment of the first benevolence ministry team. These team members had specific, limited responsibilities delegated by church leaders. The apostles had overall responsibility for leading the church. Their specific task was to "give our attention to prayer and the ministry of the word" (Acts 6:4). To a ministry team they delegated a portion of the work of the church—ministering to the widows of the Grecian Jews.

## PERSONNEL ACTIONS ADMINISTRATORS SHOULD CONSIDER

This section will focus on specific actions that church leaders should consider in order to ensure that those who carry out the functions of ministry and the support of that ministry will contribute to the security of the church. I have cited two Scripture passages that relate to the development of an organization to help carry out the mission assigned by God. Something very interesting to note in these two passages: Neither Jethro nor the apostles said, "Go out and appoint or select just anybody you spot in the street." They were looking for specific qualifications!

> Select capable men from all the people—men who fear God, trustworthy men who hate dishonest gain—and appoint them as officials over thousands, hundreds, fifties and tens. Exodus 18:21

> Choose seven men from among you who are known to be full of the Spirit and wisdom. Acts 6:3

These men not only had a job description; they had to meet certain qualifications in order to be eligible for the job.

## Develop Adequate Hiring and Employment Practices

Although I've said it once, it's important enough to say it again in a slightly different way: "It is far easier not to hire a problem employee than to have to deal with the problem after the person is employed." This process for ensuring safety and security with regard to personnel begins with a sound policy for hiring and adequate procedures to prevent the employment of an unsatisfactory worker. Here are some policy considerations a personnel committee may want to adopt:

1. Ensure that all paid ministry and support positions have job descriptions that state

- ❑ the title of the job.
- ❑ the principal function, and who does the supervision.
- ❑ the qualifications for the position.
- ❑ the specific duties or responsibilities, and which individuals, if any, they supervise.

2. Ensure that all who apply for paid ministry and support positions are considered via an application form that has as a minimum

- ❑ the applicant's full name, residence address, and means of contact (telephone, E-mail, and so forth).
- ❑ a statement that the applicant is eligible for employment in the United States. The Immigration and Naturalization Act of 1996 requires employers to complete an I–9 form and cite two forms of valid identification within seventy-two hours of employment. You do not have to cite this to make application, but the potential

The federal government provides a wealth of online information to assist churches and other organizations that must comply with the myriad of regulations concerning personnel issues. The primary site is www.firstgov.gov to access any and all United States government Web sites. (For example, by clicking on the Immigration link under the Defense and Global Affairs topical entry, information about I–9 criteria may be found on the INS—Immigration and Naturalization Service—Web site.)

employee should be aware of this requirement in case of employment.

- ❑ a statement of the applicant's self-reported qualifications for the job being applied for.
- ❑ a reasonable review of the applicant's work history—including at least the last two or three employers. Include periods of employment, duties required, and the conditions of termination, if any. Ask whether you may contact a previous employer for a comment about the applicant's work ethic.
- ❑ a statement of whether the applicant has ever been arrested for or convicted of a felony or of child or spouse abuse or molestation. A police record check should be run on all employees (paid or part-time), regardless of whether or not they will be working in proximity to children seventeen years old or younger.

Every state in the nation has a law or guideline that regulates the care and management of children. A portion of most of these state regulations is the provision that agencies providing care or direction of children to age eighteen must have access to information that would prevent the employment or use of persons who might have the potential to do harm to the child. Additionally, because of numerous lawsuits filed in recent years in cases of child abuse and child molestation in the nonprofit sector, insurance companies are not only requiring screening of these workers but also appropriate training.

Where can you go for help? Suggested resources include the following:

- The Nonprofit Risk Management Center (www.nonprofitrisk.org) provides excellent resources for organizations. Their products include the "Staff Screening Tool Kit," "Taking the High Road: A Guide to Effective and Legal Employment Practices for Nonprofits," "Child Abuse Prevention Primer for Your Organization," and "Kidding Around? Be Serious! A Commitment to Safe Service Opportunities for Young People."
- The Church Law & Tax Report of Christian Ministry Resources, Matthews, North Carolina (www.iclonline.com), has an excellent booklet and training manual titled "Reducing the Risk of Child Sexual Abuse in Your Church." Appendix 2 of that manual has information and forms to assist the church in making screening decisions.
- Commercial employee screening organizations, such as BTi Employee Screening Services of Dallas, Texas (www.btiscreening.com), provide local and nationwide comprehensive screening. The cost of this service varies, depending on the number of sources explored: criminal

continued on next page

records searches, consumer credit bureau searches, motor vehicle records searches, and education and employment verifications. These types of organizations may be identified by local authorities or diocese or parish leaders. Check to see which ones the local agency that approves day-care licenses in your area recommends.

Most denominational organizations at the national, state, and local-parish level can also provide assistance in identifying sources for screening. Check with groups within these organizations that specialize in children and youth ministry for background screening sources.

- The National Clearinghouse on Child Abuse and Neglect Information provides information about state organizations that assist groups. For example, a church in Texas may write to the Texas Department of Public Safety (Crime Records Service) or e-mail them at records.txdps.state.tx.us and ask to conduct a criminal records check. In most states a fee will be charged for each search. I recommend you go to the Web site for the attorney general in your state and search from there.

- ❑ a statement concerning whether or not the applicant is now using or has ever used any drugs or alcohol products.
- ❑ an inquiry with regard to whether the potential employee has a medical or family issue that could affect his or her ability to carry out the job functions in the expected manner. While federal and many state employment laws prevent potential employers from asking certain personal and private questions, it is perfectly legal to ask an applicant to voluntarily assess his or her employment abilities.

- ❑ a signed waiver to allow the potential employer to conduct police, credit, records, and employee history checks.

3. All volunteers who could potentially work with children (birth to age eighteen) should be screened in nearly as intense a manner as that stated above. The best way to conduct this screening is to have each person complete an application to work as a volunteer. This application would substitute "Experience Working with Children/Youth" in lieu of "Work History" in the application of point 2 above.

4. All potential employees should be interviewed. Consider two levels of interviews: (1) an initial interview to make sure that the submitted application form is complete and understandable; (2) a second interview with only the top three or four candidates for the position. This second interview should:

---

Space does not allow us to include a complete, legally defensible example of an application form. Some sources with examples include the following:

Bloss, Julie. *The Church Guide to Employment Law.* Matthews, N.C.: Christian Ministry Resources, 1993.

Frieze, Rex. *Administrative Forms Manual for Churches and Other Ministries.* Orlando, Fla.: Frieze Consulting.

Holcomb, Tim, compiler. *Personnel Administration Guide for Southern Baptist Churches.* Nashville: Convention Press, 1988.

Powers, Bruce, ed. *Church Administration Handbook.* Nashville: Broadman & Holman, 1997.

Welch, Bob. *The Church Organization Manual.* Richardson, Tex.: NACBA Publishing, 2002.

Have the legal counsel for your church review the form you create or adopt in order to ensure that it meets all the requirements of a document that could be defended in civil court.

---

Despite all these plans, anticipate problems. A friend told me a story of a former employee—someone who may now be on *your* support staff. All the safeguards for employing only appropriate individuals appeared to have been in place. A police records check had been conducted, and the person's name did not emerge as being someone of questionable character. However, three months into this person's employment, an event happened that seriously concerned the church and my friend. The church operated a day school for children six months old through kindergarten. One evening after school, my friend was walking through the hall and noticed a light on in the girls' rest room. When she entered the room, she saw that one of the toilets had plugged up and that water was flowing into the drain in the middle of the room. The janitorial crew had already left for the day. She turned off the water and went next door to the janitor's closet to find a plunger and some spray disinfectant. The closet didn't have a light, but the light from the hall lit the room enough so that she could locate the plunger and the bottle of disinfectant. Leaning in, she saw that one of the OSHA-mandated manufacturers' safety data sheets was slightly tilted, and there appeared to be a light source behind it. Moving the sheet aside, she noted a face-sized hole in the drywall and a small crack in the ceramic tile on the wall in the girls' toilet stall that would allow a person to peep into the rest room.

The next day my friend informed the headmaster and pastor of her discovery. The headmaster set about to catch the guilty party. One day he found one of the janitors in the closet with the door shut. While they never saw him with his eye to the peephole, circumstances were such

continued on next page

that his character could be questioned. He was a relatively new employee who was still within the one-year probation period. While this man was dismissed from his job, charges were not brought against him because there was no proof that he had been peeping into the girls' rest room. The hole was quickly patched and the crack plugged. A potential civil employment lawsuit was avoided because the church exercised its option for termination under the provisions of probation and did not have to demonstrate cause. Unfortunately, the individual left with no charges filed—and he may be your janitor because his name never made it into a police file.

- ❑ follow a specific pattern, asking each potential employee the same questions.
- ❑ seek clarification about information that was noted in the application.
- ❑ seek clarification about information discovered in any of the records/background checks.
- ❑ ask the individual to describe his or her character. If the position requires a theological or doctrinal stance, have the individual discuss that issue.
- ❑ ask the individual to relate how he or she can enhance the position.
- ❑ explain the requirements and qualifications for the job, and ask if the individual can meet these requirements.

5. A third interview should occur only with the individual who has been selected as the best potential applicant. During this interview, you will want to:

- ❑ make clear the requirements for the position and get the applicant's affirmation of his or her ability to achieve those expectations.
- ❑ review any employment policies and procedures and have the applicant acknowledge his or her willingness to comply.
- ❑ specifically point out any moral or character expectations. Review any theological or doctrinal requirements. Explain the consequences for the applicant's failure to conduct his or her employment within these standards.
- ❑ explain lines of authority and the applicant's role as supervisor and/or supervised.
- ❑ review compensation and benefits provided and methods for promotion.

If the individual is hired by the church, have him or her acknowledge the above items in writing.

6. I strongly suggest that all employees be hired with a provision of probation, even if the organization has declared itself an "employment at will" employer. Probation allows for a fuller background evaluation to occur and for more time for a supervisor to observe the work habits of the individual and to evaluate the potential for continued employment.

7. Bond your employees who routinely handle your funds. In recent months a church in Florida discovered that a financial secretary had been consistently taking money from the weekly offerings. The church estimated that several thousand dollars had been stolen.

This church was out the money because they had never developed audit principles that would have allowed them to

Professional personnel screening organizations usually offer evaluations of potential and current employees at several levels. Whether you use one of these professional groups or not, the personnel committee should establish the level to which a person will be screened. The following is an example:

1. All paid employees:
   - verification of name and social security number
   - verification of current and prior addresses
   - verification of previous employment
   - regional criminal records search
   - state driving records search

2. Ministerial staff:
   - all of 1 above
   - verification of qualifications/school credentials
   - credit check

3. Employees who will have unique ministry (such as counseling) or fiduciary responsibilities:
   - all of 1 and 2 above
   - expanded criminal records check to a national check

4. Volunteers who work with children and youth to age 18
   - verification of name and address
   - regional criminal records check (some churches may deem it important enough to pay the additional fee and expand to a national criminal check if the person has not lived in the local area or state for at least four or five years)

catch the thief and because they failed to carry insurance to cover such loss. Individuals such as financial secretaries, church treasurers, and all other employees who, as a part of their job responsibilities, have personal access to the church's funds should be bonded.

Insurance companies provide excellent information relating to employment dishonesty and theft coverage. Bonding will mean that a level of evaluation of the employee's background will go beyond that which is normally carried out by the personnel screening team. Insurance protection will be established to the level of potential theft—usually the total of a regular week's receipts for single loss and the potential loss between audits for employee dishonesty.

## QUESTIONS FOR REFLECTION AND DISCUSSION

I've tried to demonstrate that it is better to have in place an adequate organization and strong operational policies than to try to solve problems as they occur. In this chapter I looked at structure and procedures as being the first line of defense. At the root of nearly every personnel problem in the church lies a failure to provide the adequate leadership to prevent that problem.

As a church leader, take time to ask the following questions:

1. Is there an organizational structure within which you work? Draw a diagram of this structure. Where do you fit in? Are you the individual who must make all decisions? Or are you able to delegate to others the work of providing a secure and safe facility?

2. What type of polity decision making is used in your church? What group(s) has been delegated the responsibility of providing a safe and secure worship, study, and ministry environment? Who is their staff liaison? How do you stay informed of their activities?

3. Do you screen all applicants for positions of service and ministry? If you use an application form, review it according to the considerations discussed in this chapter. If you don't use one, create one based on the guidance you've received in this chapter.

4. What are at least three resources you could use to help you screen an applicant for working with and around children in your church?

# THREE

## Taking Actions to Improve Security

A prudent man sees danger and takes refuge,
but the simple keep going and suffer for it.
PROVERBS 22:3; 27:12

Twice the writer of Proverbs warns that it is the prudent person who makes plans when danger is present. Writing to the church leaders, Peter admonishes them to "Be shepherds of God's flock that is under your care, serving as overseers—not because you must, but because you are willing, as God wants you to be; not greedy for money, but eager to serve; not lording it over those entrusted to you, but being examples to the flock" (1 Peter 5:2–3). The prudent shepherd provides a secure pasture for the sheep, knowing that quiet waters are nearby. The shepherd leads the sheep and with a rod and staff protects them from danger and from the enemy—analogy taken from Psalm 23.

In the first two chapters I've considered some preparatory activities that can be accomplished to provide a secure environment for worship and ministry. The watchword was that it is better to solve the problem before it occurs than to have to deal with it later. Unfortunately, many church leaders don't have the luxury of making and carrying out plans to construct a security-conscious building but have to live with what they already have. Similarly, not all churches have seriously thought through their personnel practices to ensure that security issues are being considered in their hiring strategies and in the creation of an organization to carry out ministry.

These final two chapters will address many issues relating to security that can be put in place, regardless of the status or condition of the church. Many of these suggestions apply even to the smallest of churches.

## INVENTORY EQUIPMENT AND FURNISHINGS

At one time or another you've read of a church employee or volunteer worker who embezzled money over a period of time. More often than not, the cause of the loss was a combination of an unlimited trust in the individual and poor financial audit procedures. While this type of loss can be sensational news, let me tell you of a loss just as insidious. I was the administrator of a fast-growing large church. We had a well-organized property committee and a set of excellent policies and procedures that outlined the use of the facility and its furnishings. The committee had decided that all major plant equipment and all electronics needed to be inventoried—both for accountability and maintenance reasons. We had a zillion tables and chairs, but it was decided that those didn't need to be inventoried. About every other month my building superintendent would come with a request for fifty or so new folding chairs. At first I thought nothing about it, since we were growing and undoubtedly needed them. One time, when I asked him why he needed more chairs, he commented that there weren't enough to meet the seating plans the minister of education had designated for each room. To make a long story short, the building superintendent and I soon did an inventory. A couple months later we did another inventory and found that in that two-month period nearly thirty-five chairs had vanished. We discovered, much to our embarrassment, that one of the night janitors had been taking chairs home, one at a time, and selling them to the used-furniture stores and junk shops in the area. We had made two mistakes: (1) We hadn't adequately marked the chairs as belonging to the church, and (2) we hadn't inventoried them. We changed our procedures to correct both errors.

One of the principal reasons items are stolen is because we are careless about their care. The church has entrusted to ministry leaders the stewardship of the church property. One of the first acts to help deter theft is to *make items unattractive to a thief.*

- ❑ Develop a policy statement to delineate what property is to be inventoried. This may be by item, cost, or degree of loss potential.
- ❑ Record the name and location of each piece of property.
- ❑ If available, list source, date of purchase, price, and any warranty information.
- ❑ Create a format—such as an Excel spreadsheet—on a computer system to record dates of inventory and changes.
- ❑ Conduct inventories at least annually. Update files and records. Record the date of each inventory.
- ❑ Take a picture or do a videotaping of the item. If a digital image is created, add it to the computer database.
- ❑ Where appropriate, mark the items as belonging to you.
    - ❖ Use an etching pencil or marker to inscribe the name of the church.
    - ❖ Purchase labels that can be attached to the equipment. Select a label that has an excellent adhesive and cannot be removed easily.

- ❖ Do not hide your mark. Let others see that the item belongs to you.
- ❏ Always create a backup of an inventory file and place in a secure location, such as a bank safety deposit vault.

A sample inventory record and file is found in my book titled *The Church Organization Manual,* which can be ordered from the National Association of Church Business Administration online at www.nacba.net. Order the CD version and get ready-made forms in which you may insert your church's name and any changes you want to make to the form without worry of copyright infringement. Another excellent resource for church forms is the *Administrative Forms Manual* by Rex Frieze, which can be ordered from the author at www.friezeconsulting.com. Use of these forms requires permission from the author.

## CONDUCT AN ANNUAL AUDIT

Audits perform two important functions. First, they ensure that the assets of the church or organization are being adequately and appropriately cared for, and second, they enable the stewards of church property to state to the congregation that the stewardship they have been entrusted with is being carried out—in other words, audits protect the church and her members.

### Develop a Policy Statement

Develop a policy statement that calls for an audit of church resources every year. Ensure that the audit evaluates the policies and procedures for handling money from the moment it leaves a parishioner's hand through the counting, recording, and posting of the contributions and finally on to the expenditures of funds. Some procedural elements might include using a checklist that asks the following questions:

### FINANCIAL ACCOUNTABILITY SECURITY CHECKLIST

- ✔ Do at least two ushers collect and take contributions to the counting space?
- ✔ Is there a secure counting room?
- ✔ Are at least two members of a counting team present at all times during a count?
- ✔ Are counting team members unrelated to each other?
- ✔ Do counting team members routinely rotate in order to prevent the same persons from always counting funds?
- ✔ Are funds in an envelope confirmed with the amount listed on the envelope? If the amount isn't listed there, make sure someone accurately records it on the giving envelope.
- ✔ Are checks dated appropriately and immediately endorsed?
- ✔ Is all cash double counted?
- ✔ Is a second copy of the deposit slip given to the administrator, pastor, treasurer, or another person who had nothing to do with the counting of funds?
- ✔ Are funds transported in a locked container?
- ✔ Are funds immediately taken to a secure location or to a bank by two individuals?
- ✔ Are funds placed in the bank verified against the counting team deposit slip?
- ✔ Are offering envelopes and a copy of the deposit slip given to a person who is responsible for recording the individual giving of the membership?
- ✔ Are funds received during the week receipted for by at least two accountable individuals?
- ✔ Regardless of the accounting method used by the treasurer or financial secretary, are the funds posted so an accurate depiction of funds available, funds obligated, and funds expended is given?

- ✔ Is a purchase order system used to request and obligate expenditures from funds? Does this system have limits that a single individual or program head may approve?
- ✔ Is there a balance sheet system to reconcile funds received, funds obligated, materials or resources received, and payments made?
- ✔ Is there at least a monthly statement of the accounts reported to the church?

### Form an Audit Team

Form an audit team made up of members of the finance committee and members from the church at large—a total of three to five members should be sufficient. Let this team function for three years. During each of the first two years the team itself conducts the audit. In year three the team contracts with an outside audit firm to conduct the audit, after which the team implements the recommendations by the outside audit group.

## FORM AN EMERGENCY REACTION TEAM (ERT)

One Sunday during the morning worship service a distraction occurred on the far side of the sanctuary. The pastor paused right in the middle of his sermon and asked us to bow in prayer for this member who needed assistance. Two ushers had noted that one of our members was having breathing problems. They had moved quietly down the aisle and helped the man lie down. A moment later a young woman came down the aisle and began to aid the individual. She placed an aspirin under his tongue, loosened his clothing, and monitored his pulse rate. The two ushers returned with another person who was toting a folding stretcher and a blanket. In a few moments they took the man out to a waiting ambulance called by the two ushers who had made a quick stop to use the phone at the welcome center in the foyer.

Happy endings are always nice. This church member had suffered a heart attack. The two ushers—trained to help a person in distress—initially aided him and then went to the welcome center to call fire department EMS personnel. A predetermined signal had been sounded in the church, and a member who was a nurse responded by caring for the man until a stretcher—purchased from a surplus store—could be brought to remove the individual to a place where care could be administered. The ambulance arrived at the correct door and was met by one of the persons who had taken care of the individual from the very beginning of the episode. The man survived the heart attack and was able to attend worship services within a few weeks.

Most churches will have within their membership individuals who have training or experience in responding to emergency situations. These may be law enforcement officials, fire department members, medical personnel, military personnel, or other individuals who can come together to provide leadership in these situations. In addition to the case cited above, our ERT has responded to choking children, cuts and falls, and even the shard of an entry door's broken glass buried in a child's back. We used our ERT to train children's workers and to teach our youth to do cardiopulmonary resuscitation (CPR).

Here are several suggestions to aid in putting together an effective emergency reaction team:

❑ Identify a primary leader who can organize the team to ensure that someone is always present when the church is gathered for worship or other meetings.

- ❑ Agree that the team's principal function will be to provide immediate intermediary care or action until municipal authorities respond.
- ❑ Develop a method of signaling the team into action. In my church we used the Sunday school buzzer. Some churches give team members a local area pager, and I know of one church that uses a cell phone paging system.
- ❑ Provide primary emergency response equipment—stretchers, blankets, breathing support, and the like—the type of equipment team members have been trained to use.
- ❑ Establish a liaison with local emergency (fire, police, ambulance) authorities to establish a recognized pattern of response to an emergency:
    - ❖ Locate and identify primary doors where personnel and equipment may meet ERT personnel, who can then be directed to the site of the emergency.
    - ❖ Establish a protocol for responding to questions typically asked by the local area 911 or other emergency receiving system.
    - ❖ Organize and carry out training for ERT personnel by these authorities.

## PROVIDE ADEQUATE LIGHTING OUTSIDE THE BUILDING

Law enforcement officials will tell you that the greatest deterrent to crime is providing a lighted area. By providing lighting to the building exterior, two objectives are met: (1) The lights will illuminate the area, making it safe for your parishioners and visitors to move around, and (2) the lights will deter the physical intrusion into the building of those who have no business entering.

When discussing lighting, we need to understand a couple of general terms:

Illumination, or light level, is measured in **foot-candles** *(ft-c)*.

Light output from the source is measured in **lumens-per-watt** *(l/w)*.

## Illuminate the Parking Lot

The chart on page 62 shows that high pressure sodium (hps) provides the most economical lighting. These lights have dominant red, yellow, and orange spectrum light output; as a result,

**STANDARDS FOR ILLUMINATION**

| **Area Illuminated** | ***ft-c*** |
|---|---|
| Choir | 30-70* |
| Pulpit | 50-100* |
| Worship area | 15-30* |
| Offices | 50 |
| Classrooms | 50 |
| Halls/lobby/foyer | 10 |
| Gyms/auditoriums | 5-15 |
| Parking lots | 1-3 |

*Higher levels of illumination are needed if television or video production is to take place.

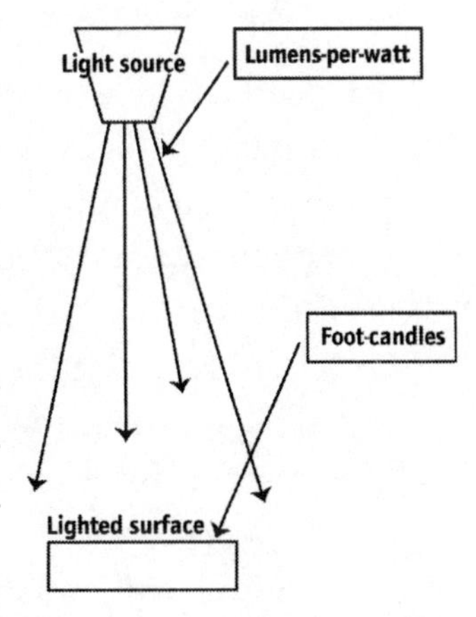

**SAMPLE LIGHT SOURCES**

| Light source | Small Size* | Medium Size* | Large Size* |
|---|---|---|---|
| High pressure sodium (hps) | 84 | 105 | 126 |
| Metal halide (mh) | 67 | 75 | 93 |
| Fluorescent (fl) | 66 | 74 | 70 |
| Mercury vapor (mv) | 44 | 51 | 57 |
| Incandescent (i) | 17 | 22 | 24 |

*Bulb size and ballast

they penetrate fog, rain, and other light-refracting conditions. The downside is that the color renditions (the way color appears to the eye) are poor. The human eye prefers the white light of the halide, fluorescent, and mercury fixtures. The following suggestions for placement focus on efficiency features as well as on the need to provide adequate, secure lighting.

- ❑ Place high pressure sodium (hps) lights around the perimeter of the parking lot. Because these lights stay on longer, you'll appreciate the higher efficiency rating for cost-effectiveness. Perimeter lights may be turned off at an appropriate late hour, or they may be left on all night.
- ❑ Place metal halide (mh) or mercury (mv) lights within the parking lot itself. These lights will be utilized only when the parking lot is being used by parishioners. The white lights will provide pleasing visibility as they illuminate the lot. Additionally, they will merge color spectrum with the entrance lights discussed in the next section.

- ❑ Provide lighting to the parking lot at a minimum level of *2ft-c.* (Many insurance companies encourage you to provide parking lot illumination to *3ft-c.*) The measure of light will vary according to several factors:

  - ❖ the light source—the choice of bulb type and size. For example, using information from the tables above, it would take two mercury bulbs to provide the same light as a sodium source. One medium-sized metal halide bulb provides the same illumination as three incandescent bulbs of the same wattage.
  - ❖ the lighted surface—concrete reflects light; asphalt and gravel absorb light.
  - ❖ the height of the lights—for example, a 1000-watt hps light placed at 35 feet above the ground will provide *2ft-c* average illumination in a 200-foot circle; at 40 feet above the ground the light only provides 1.5*ft-c* of average illumination in the same area.

Tables of illumination for a variety of light sources are available from lighting distributors, electrical engineers, and local power companies, and they can be found in library resources and at online sites as well. Light sources are constantly being improved, so if you are planning to modify your parking lot lighting, you are encouraged to get the latest information from professional lighting experts. The Federal Energy Management Program (www.energy.gov) and the National Energy Foundation (www.nef1.org) are two excellent places to begin research into energy conservation. You'll also find helpful book resources at your local library, including Kao Chen's *Energy Management in Illuminating Systems* (Boca Raton, Fla: CRC Press,

1999) and Albert Thumann's *Lighting Efficiency Application* (Lilburn, Ga.: Fairmont Press, 1991).

## Illuminate the Entrances to the Facility

The illumination around the church's entrance points is one of the primary considerations for security and safety. As I noted in chapter 1, most violations of entrance to the church occur at the designated points of opening, namely, doors and windows. If you've ever stood in a dark doorway and fumbled for your keys, you know what I'm saying. Bright, well-lit entrances not only make a welcoming statement, but they also provide security.

Here are a few things to keep in mind with regard to entrance lighting:

- ❑ Ensure that a minimum of 10 foot-candles of lighting illuminates both the entrance and any foyer, as well as a portico or covered entryway.
- ❑ Use white-spectrum (metal halide, fluorescent, mercury vapor, or incandescent) lights.
- ❑ Place the lighting on a photocell so that the entrances and foyers are illuminated whenever it is dark.
- ❑ Consider using low-voltage fluorescent lighting for maximum cost-effectiveness. From the charts above, note the advantages of using fluorescent lights—gaining the same amount of light as three incandescent bulbs of the same wattage. Low voltage means lower costs, as well as longer bulb life. The initial higher cost of this type of fixture will pay for itself in cost savings very early in the life of its use.
- ❑ Always place dual-bulb fixtures in order to ensure that the area is illuminated if one of the bulbs should burn out.

- ❑ Use durable, vandal-resistant fixtures. Look for fixtures that are rated "high-abuse lighting" or that have lens covers of polycarbonate plastic. Lighting fixtures should be affixed with tamper-resistant or security attachments. While these fixtures may be more expensive than standard installation types, their durability and the security they provide pay off in the long run.
- ❑ Position light switches in secure locations. An ideal wiring scheme is to directly wire the lights from the circuit panel via a photocell. The photocell should be mounted exterior to the building in an elevated, secure location.

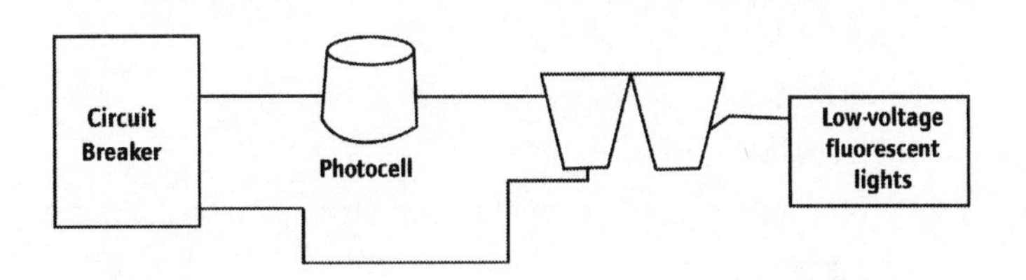


## Illuminate around the Perimeter of the Building

Architects often design down/up lighting around buildings as part of the structure's architectural statement. While their intent is to highlight features of the design, such lighting can be used effectively for security. Here are some suggestions for perimeter lighting:

- ❑ Use low-voltage lighting systems for maximum cost-effectiveness. From the charts above, note that fluorescent lighting systems provide as much light per watt as the metal halides and more than the mercury vapors.

Because of the long life of the fixture, fluorescent lamps are the most cost-effective.

❑ Down lighting from eaves provides the most secure method of providing illumination, because it is elevated and out of reach. Down lighting requires less expensive

The time period in which lights are on can be easily controlled via a simple wiring scheme:

- From the power source place a timer that will energize the circuit at a preset time (for example, at 4:00 P.M.). This "on time" never has to be changed, regardless of the season of the year or time change (standard time or daylight saving time).
- On the load side of the timer place a photocell that will energize the circuit at dusk.
- The lights come on when the timer and photocell have both energized the lights.
- Set the timer to turn off the circuit at a preset time. This may be a designated time (for example, at midnight) or when the lighting is no longer required as determined by the church schedule.

These lighting schemes are useful for perimeter and parking lot lights that do not need to be on continually throughout the night.

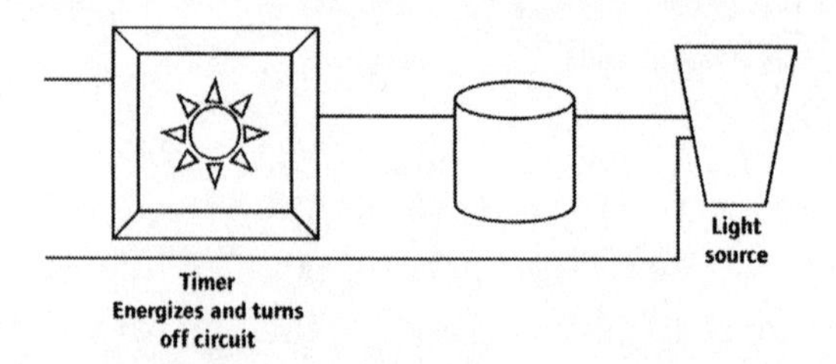

fixtures. The ground fixtures that provide up lighting must be waterproof and require a greater degree of tamper-resistant qualities—all of which adds to the cost.

- ❑ Perimeter illumination should be considered for all walled surfaces that have ground-level windows.
- ❑ Depending on the level of security desired, lights may be left on during all periods of darkness or placed on a timer cutoff. (See sidebar on page 66 for more information on timers.)

## USE LANDSCAPE TO PREVENT SURREPTITIOUS ENTRY INTO THE BUILDING

Take a walk around your church facility, and ask these two questions:

1. If someone were to try to enter the building through a window or door, would shrubbery and trees hide his or her activity from view?

2. Could a person be hiding in bushes near an entrance and spring out to attack someone entering or leaving the building?

There are some simple steps you can take if you answered yes to these questions. You probably don't have to hire a landscape architect to resolve your problems:

- ❑ Trim—and keep trimmed—any bushes or shrubs to a point below the level of the windowsill. If you need to replace any bushes, consider putting in low, slow-growing evergreen plants. Plants have different levels of hardiness, depending on which part of the country you live in, so you'd be wise to consult a local nursery or read the labels of plants to determine their hardiness, whether they are deciduous or evergreen, and what their mature height will be.

- ❑ Remove plantings around entrances and replace with very low-lying landscape features. Many churches place a bench or decorative urns near their entrances. Vine or ground covers can provide pleasing color and can soften the area as well. The objective is to remove any potential hiding place close to a doorway.
- ❑ Plant trees or tall shrubs in greenbelts or islands at least ten feet from the building itself. A greater distance from the building may be desirable if the tree at maturity would have the potential to provide a second-floor access to the building.

## ORGANIZE YOUR USHERS TO BE SENSITIVE TO SECURITY

I was once a member of a church that had a high-profile, somewhat controversial pastor. It was necessary to provide a level of security for him that doesn't have to be provided for most pastors. Some of my seminary students were part of the security force. They were not uniformed guards, but well-dressed young men who stood at the doors of the church and greeted members and visitors alike. During the service they looked like dutiful seminary students, sitting on the front rows of each aisle of the church. And at invitation time (don't forget, I'm Baptist!) they were part of the group of "welcoming commitment" counselors. What no one noticed was the small tubular probe neatly tucked up each man's sleeve—a metal detector. As you entered the sanctuary, they "scanned" you. If you came down the aisle, they greeted you and "scanned" you. Seated in the balcony were some security types who could talk to the "ushers" via an earphone that looked like a standard hearing aid.

In no way am I suggesting that your church needs to develop such an elaborate system of detecting problems. However, by using an existing usher ministry team, security inside the place of worship can be enhanced.

## Train Your Ushers to Recognize Visitors

An usher or greeter ministry team can get to know who are regularly attending members of the church and who are visitors. My student Jeff Laster told me that one of the reasons he approached Larry Ashbrook was because he knew he wasn't a member of Wedgwood Baptist Church. The young men in my former church would engage "visitors" in conversation to get to know something about them, listening for words of animosity or anger. Train your ushers to be friendly but also to listen for some warning signs. Ashbrook asked, "Is this where those Christians are meeting?" The question itself and the tone of his voice probably were pretty good clues that he hadn't come to join in worship.

## Ask Your Ushers to Stay on Duty

Usher responsibilities do not end the moment the choir walks in and the pastor calls the church to worship. Ushers should remain alert throughout the service to respond to any problems that arise or to meet needs of the worshipers. Whether it is helping a mom with a toddler find a rest room, responding to a worshiper who is having a heart attack, or being the first to leap into action when disturbances occur, the usher's job continues throughout the time of gathering. (By the way, ushers often are part of the ERT—see page 58.)

Being alert for all these contingencies requires training—a training that can in many cases be obtained from diocese or regional leaders. Some local law enforcement offices provide a community relations officer who can teach ushers how to identify and deal with problem individuals.

## Assign Certain Ushers to Patrol the Facility

Some ushers should be assigned to wander around the facility during services. If the children and youth areas do not already have a designated "hall monitor," an usher should be in those areas on a routine basis. They should stop and chat with any adult who does not appear to have a legitimate reason to be in the area. Roving ushers should check on the security of the office, choir room, council room, and other areas where the need for security is great. You may want to provide these ushers with a two-way radio communication tool for added security and response capability.

## Guidelines for Ushers Who Collect the Offering

In many churches, ushers will be assigned the responsibility to receive the offering from the worshipers. A minimum of two individuals should be present at all times when handling money. Two ushers should take the offering to the counting room, where there will be a minimum of two individuals who will count the money.

## TRAIN THE GREETER MINISTRY TEAM TO BE SECURITY CONSCIOUS

In many churches, from the time someone pulls into a church parking lot to the time he or she sits in a Bible study class or a worship service, they are welcomed by individuals who provide whatever assistance is needed. This greeter ministry team can be a valuable part of your security plan.

Parking lot greeters provide security for cars and the individuals in those cars. During services they provide a level of deterrence to prevent vandalism and theft. After services they

---

Many communities require churches to identify their parking lots as private property that is subject to the limitations the property owner places on the lot. This has both legal and liability ramifications. Whether or not a sign is required, the property *is* private property, and you (the church) are held accountable for what goes on there. Check with your attorney, but a sign with a statement that reads something like this might be an appropriate safeguard:

**This parking lot is the private property of XYZ Community Church and is designated for the use of its members and visitors to the church.**

**Violators of the use of this property and of the vehicles legally parked herein by church members and visitors to church services and activities will be prosecuted to the fullest extent of the law.**

---

provide for the security of individuals as they move to their vehicles—especially during the evening hours. Here are some tips to help make their ministry more effective:

- ❑ Provide a means of identification for these folks. An orange traffic-control vest, a baseball cap, or a name badge will assist visitors—and all who drive into the parking lot—to identify these persons as representatives of the church.
- ❑ Make it possible for parking lot greeters to stay in communication with the church. A two-way radio with a home base station at the welcome center is used in some churches.
- ❑ If your parking lot is large, consider the use of electric golf carts. Some churches will use larger, multiperson carts to transport individuals to the church entrances if requested or if appropriate. Some put a flashing yellow light on top of the cart to serve as a security warning.
- ❑ Provide a system of rotation for your parking lot greeters so that no single individual has to endure inclement weather for long periods of time.

## PROVIDE IDENTIFICATION TO INDIVIDUALS

Demographers and church growth researchers state that, at any one time in a church, the average member will know closely only about a dozen individuals, will become familiar with about fifty others, and will recognize maybe a few dozen more. Thus, the larger a church, the harder it is to keep up with who people are. Identification becomes a critical issue in several venues of church ministry.

## Identify Greeters, Ushers, and Other Staff Members

When I worked at Ace Hardware for a brief period of time, customers would ask me questions because I wore a red vest. When we walk through the aisles at WalMart, we look for the blue-vested person for assistance. A policeman in uniform is easily identified as an authority we can look to for aid or assistance. Give those who provide assistance and support in our churches' ministry some sort of badge that is readily recognized. An orange vest for a parking lot greeter, a name badge for a welcome greeter, and a flower for an usher all help to identify them as persons who can assist others.

## Identify the Persons Authorized to Work with Children

Parents are reluctant to hand over their "bundle of joy" to just anyone. They want to be assured that the person who takes responsibility for the child is (1) authorized by the church to do so and (2) recognized as capable of taking care of the little one just as competently as the parent would. An identification name badge says that

- ❑ the church has reviewed the character of this person via a background check.
- ❑ the church has trained this person to properly care for and minister to children.
- ❑ the church has conducted required training for child abuse and child molestation identification and prevention.
- ❑ this person is authorized to be in this space (how else would a roving usher know who is supposed to be there?).

The use of a different type (or color) of badge can serve to identify temporary or provisional workers until they meet all qualifications. It also signals that whenever this provisional worker is spending time around children, he or she should be in the company of another adult who has met all the criteria.

## Create a Way to Identify Children

One of the reasons children ministry leaders state for having no more than a handful of children per worker is that it is hard to keep up with a greater number. In recent years we've heard horror stories about churches that have been sued because a child had been taken by someone who wasn't authorized to take him or her. In one case a dad came to the child care area after a service and asked to pick up his toddler. When the little one identified this man as "Daddy," the worker released the child. A few minutes later the mother came in, only to discover that the child had been given to the father—a man whom the courts had barred from coming near the child without law enforcement supervision.

Here are some ways churches can protect themselves and their parishioners:

### *Information Cards*

Have an information card completed for every child. This card should identify

- ❑ the name of the child.
- ❑ a list of persons who are authorized to receive the child.
- ❑ a list of any medications or pertinent medical history.
- ❑ the place where the parents can be reached during the time the workers are caring for the child.

Some churches attach a statement of inoculations, certification that a child is free from any communicable disease, and the like.

*Identification Tags*

Attach an identification tag or badge that identifies who each child is. Attach the same identification to all his or her possessions. Younger children will want to "play" with their tag, so find some simple scheme that does not attract their attention. Older children will wear their tag with pride.

This tag or identification system becomes the way parents are identified as those who can legitimately pick up the child. Churches have adopted some ingenious methods down through the years. Some use a scan card system, others issue local area pagers, while others use a matching interlocking badge. I love the cartoon of the baby with the bar-coded diaper that is swiped across a grocery store type of scanner. The objective in all of these identification methods is to return the child to the parent or guardian—and *only* to that parent or guardian—who is authorized to receive the child.

*The new technology led to greater efficiency at First Church.*

***Training and Resources***

Conduct all your training with a view to ensuring the protection of the child. If your church is sued for neglect in the care of a child—especially in molestation situations—your defense will have to include evidence that you carried out "all reasonable measures" to protect the child, including having provided training for individuals who take care of children.

Churches have lost lawsuits because they were shown to be negligent in their efforts to provide a safe and secure environment for children and youth. Courts have required that there be appropriate training at least annually—in addition to initial screening and background checks of workers in children's ministry. In response, insurance carriers have made adequate training a part of their requirement for liability coverage in this area, and many provide training materials to assist their clients. State and local agencies that regulate child care and child protection have also developed training materials that are available to assist the church. Your denominational or diocese headquarters is another good place to look for resources.

Christian Ministry Resources (located in Matthews, North Carolina) offers excellent resources for assistance in this area—the Church Law and Tax Report's *Reducing the Risk of Child Sexual Abuse in Your Church* by Richard Hammar, Steven Klipowicz, and James Cobble (two-part video, audio cassette, training manual, and reference book) is one of the best. Another admirable resource is Ernest Zarra's *It Should Never Happen Here: A Guide for Minimizing the Risk of Child Abuse in Ministry* (Grand Rapids: Baker, 1997).

## QUESTIONS FOR REFLECTION AND DISCUSSION

In chapter 2 I noted that the concept of an *organization* is extremely important in assisting the leadership of the church in providing for security. In this chapter I've introduced several activities that call on church leaders to develop various facets of their organizational structure to meet security needs. In assessing your church's capability for providing a secure facility, work through the following questions:

1. Does your church have adequate lighting to provide safe and secure movement from an individual's vehicle to the church facility?

   To help you make this assessment, draw a sketch of your entire facility—property and all. Mark where the exterior lights exist. Mark where door lighting exists. Then some evening after it has turned completely dark outside, go into the parking lot with your Bible. Open it, and take a careful look. Can you read the print? If so, you probably have enough light. If not, you may want to consider adding light. Do the same test at your entryways.

2. Do your ushers and greeters have the necessary skills to respond to emergencies? How would they respond if a Larry Ashbrook walked into your church? Would they be prepared to deal with any medical emergencies that may occur during a worship service? Who walks around your facility during meetings to ensure security?

   If you have other questions that you're not sure how to answer, you may want to consider developing a ministry team to help you with security issues. Who would be the ideal person to head up such a program? Buy him or her a copy of this book. Write down the issues you'd like to discuss once he or she has read the book.

# FOUR

# Dealing with Keys, Alarms, and Security Systems

One afternoon as two deacons and I were looking over some areas of the church, we came across a locked room. I had left my key ring in the office, so I asked them to wait for a moment while I ran down to my office to get my keys. "Don't bother," they replied in unison. "I have a master key." Now I had just completed twenty-two years of service in the Navy, where no one except a small handful of people had master keys. Much to my surprise I soon learned that just about anybody in the church had a master key. In the next budget request, I suggested that we include a line item for rekeying the church. It cost us a couple thousand dollars for a locksmith, but I gained control over the key control problem.

## ESTABLISH KEY CONTROL

- ❏ Create a policy statement that dictates who gets what keys to what areas. The policy statement is an important first step. It is easier to say, "You don't have a need for that key, because our policy permits only _____ individuals to have those keys," when you have a written policy in effect.
- ❏ Establish a sign-out/return log for all keys. Know how many keys of all types you have and where they are.
- ❏ Create a limited number of master keys and have them stamped "Do Not Duplicate." Legitimate locksmiths will honor this mark on a key.
- ❏ If funds permit, key locked areas by zone so that a submaster key will open a number of doors in a specific

area. Recreation areas, educational spaces, music spaces, school spaces, and entry doors are some examples. A grand master will open all spaces; submasters will open doors only in the designated area. Area submaster keys should also be marked "Do Not Duplicate."

- ❑ Control how you issue the keys in order to reduce to a bare minimum the number of keys required by an individual to perform his or her responsibilities. Some examples are noted below:

---

**Employees of a Christian Academy**

- The church administrator has a grand master that opens all doors of the church.
- The headmaster has a submaster for all spaces used by the academy.
- Teachers have keys for their particular rooms.

**Those Who Work at a Church's Recreation Center**

- The church administrator has a grand master that opens all doors of the church.
- The minister of recreation has a submaster to all recreation/family life center spaces.
- Sports equipment volunteers are given a key to areas where equipment is stored.
- Volunteer counselors are given a key to recreation areas.
- Volunteer teachers are given a key to craft areas.
- Food service personnel have keys to the kitchen and storage areas.

**Custodians and Janitors**

- The church administrator has a master key to all spaces.
- The building supervisor or lead janitor is given an entrance key and a submaster to all spaces he or she is assigned to clean.
- Custodians are not given any keys; they rely on the supervisor to grant entry into any locked room or area as appropriate.

---

Consider the use of electronic keys. Electronic keying systems generally come in two formats: (1) a keypad punch system that requires the person who desires entry to know a specific series of numbers to actuate an electric bolt or to unlatch a manual dead bolt, and (2) a magnetic card inserted into the locking system, which senses a correct alignment of codes and then releases the bolt system. While these systems are expensive, they can be useful and cost-effective when

- ❑ your locking system is often compromised.
- ❑ it is necessary to change the locks frequently.
- ❑ a variety of individuals require entry to the space, but the list of individuals changes frequently.
- ❑ you want to allow a group of individuals into a specific area of the church but not into other areas that have key systems (for example, a prayer room).
- ❑ you want to secure a space beyond the level of security a master key system provides. For example, someone may have a master key that allows entry into an office area, but they cannot enter the financial records secretary's office without knowing the electronic code on the special lock on that door.

An advantage to electronic or magnetic locking systems is that they can be actuated and monitored from a remote central security system.

## INSTALL ALARM SYSTEMS TO DETER INTRUDERS

A church administrator came to me one day with a perplexing problem. Someone was routinely breaking into the church.

Not much would be taken; more often than not they'd simply raid the kitchen for food to eat and then sleep in the facility. She had an idea who it was, because some evenings she would observe several individuals, who appeared to be migrant workers, sitting in a car parked across the street. Her church had an alarm system, but, like most churches, it was not a general intrusion system but was targeted to the more important areas of the church.

I told her that I had had the same problem several years ago and had solved it in a unique way. My son was the canine officer of a local law enforcement group in our community. I related the problem to him, and he said, "Why don't we let Breston [the dog] wander through the building at night to see if he could sniff out the intruders." It seemed like a good idea to me, so for the next few nights we'd come in after midnight, shut off the alarm system, and turn the dog loose. Every once in a while we'd hear Breston barking—and then loud noises (usually the breaking of windows as people scampered away to escape the dog). Apparently the word got around, because the visitors soon stopped using the church as a motel.

My friend thought this was a good idea, so she arranged for a friend who owned a German Shepherd to allow the dog to roam the church for the next several weeks. She kept a light on in the foyer so the dog could be seen from time to time (she put a food bowl there also). This worked pretty well—until she started having to clean up the "love offerings" left by the dog. She went to plan B, which was to keep the light on and the dog bowl in the foyer, but to set up a tape recorder that occasionally played the sounds of a barking dog over the intercom. Interesting alarm system!

Security systems do not prevent intrusion; they deter it from happening, detect it when it happens, and report it to responding authorities. Good security systems are not cheap, but they are well worth the money spent. Here are some things to consider when placing a security system in your facility:

- ❑ Make security system features (wiring, latches, sensors, and so forth) part of any new construction or remodeling project. As I've observed in chapter 1, it is much cheaper to build in features than to retrofit.
- ❑ Plan to wire an alarm for only the critical areas of the church facility. Here is where your security ministry team or work group and your insurance agent can be of great assistance. Most major insurance companies have risk management experts who can help you identify important areas in the church for alarm systems. Sound and music system areas, offices, and major equipment areas are often designated. If your insurance representative can't help you, ask your local law enforcement agency community relations officer.
- ❑ Alarm sensors should be placed in such a manner that the sensor itself and the wiring or antennae system are tamper-proof. To achieve this entails running the wiring in the frame of the door or window and embedding the sensors in the jambs. Motion sensors should be high enough to prevent blocking and also have any wiring embedded in the wall or ceiling. Radio/wireless systems have the advantage of not having extensive runs of wiring.
- ❑ Ensure that monitors, keypad activators and disablers, and other control mechanisms are in secure locations.

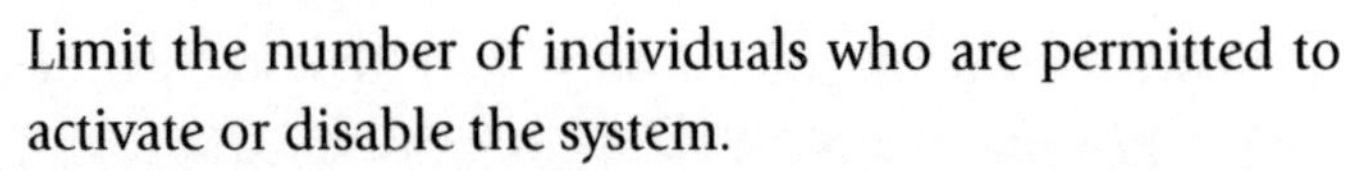

Limit the number of individuals who are permitted to activate or disable the system.

- ❑ Alarm systems should have backup power supplies in the event of a power outage.
- ❑ When the codes are changed, make sure that all persons who have access know about it. This is not the best way for the local police department to get to know your pastor!
- ❑ It is senseless to have an alarm system without a reliable response network. Be sure to ask the alarm supplier about their methods of responding to the system:
  - ❖ Do they have a response unit?
  - ❖ Do they notify cognizant municipal law enforcement or emergency authorities?
  - ❖ Do they notify designated persons from the church?
  - ❖ How many false alarms do they allow?
- ❑ Create an integrated alarm system. Most reliable alarm companies will integrate a variety of alarm modules in the installed system. In this way one system can monitor intrusion; fire, gas, and water detection; and panic alarms.

---

Depending on the type of alarm sounded, most reliable alarm systems will automatically notify police, sheriff department, and fire department or emergency medical personnel. Many municipal organizations now have a limit on the number of false alarms they will respond to before the church will be assessed a fee. This topic needs to be discussed thoroughly with the security alarm supplier and municipal authorities.

---

Make sure the company has a method of distinguishing between the different types of emergency.

- ❑ Install some nonresponse alarm detection devices to deter intrusion. One problem I discovered in law enforcement personnel's response to an intrusion alarm was that they were reluctant to enter the church until a church staff member arrived. The principal reason was because they didn't know where the light switches were, and they weren't inclined to wander around in a dark building. With this in mind, we made three modifications that were greatly appreciated:

  1. We installed a "night light" in all hallways. A low-voltage, low-wattage light was placed in the center of every hallway. Even when the main hallway lights were out, there was approximately 2 foot-candles of light in the hall.
  2. We installed twenty-four-hour lighted "exit" signs with a white light down-light lens at the ends of each hallway. LED exit light systems are low voltage and consume minimum amounts of light. Exit signs are required by code; simply buy the ones with the white light feature.
  3. We installed a motion detector in the hallway. Many schools and institutions have begun to use these. The switch stays on, and if the sensor does not detect movement after a set period of time, the lights go off. With this system in place, I—or a police officer—can walk throughout the building and not worry about

turning hall lights on or off. It also serves to startle and scare away intruders.

The diagram below demonstrates a typical hallway with these features.

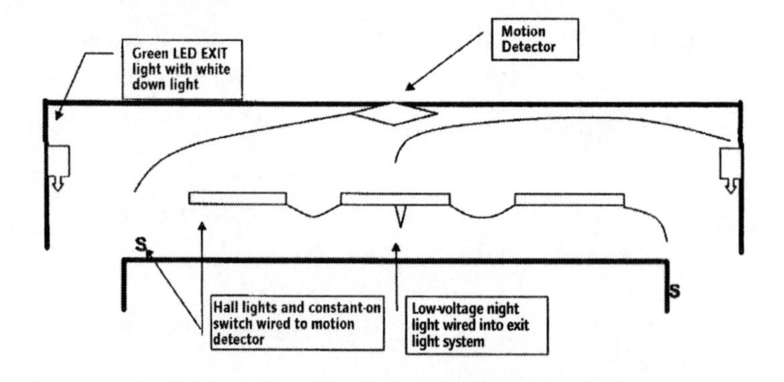


❑ Install panic alarms. This type of alarm is quite prevalent nowadays. Under the counter of many bank tellers is a small button that can be pushed in the event of a robbery. On the keyboard of most home alarm systems is a red panic button the homeowner can push to summon help, regardless of the type of emergency. Many elderly persons now carry some type of radio system that can summon help. Most phones sold today have a one-button 911 calling system. Here are some suggestions for placement in your church (bear in mind that a telephone should be in close proximity to each place where a panic alarm has been installed):

- the office area at the receptionist's desk
- the financial secretary's office

- the welcome/receiving area or office areas in the preschool and children's wing
- the money-counting room
- your parking lot (if you have a very large one)—consider marking these panic alarms with a blue light
- the welcome center or area where your ERT assembles

## INSTALL A SECURITY CAMERA SYSTEM AS A DETERRENT

Video cameras have been used for many years as an integral part of security systems in many businesses, stores, and municipal buildings. While cameras do not completely stop crime, their presence does serve as a deterrent. Until recently, the use of camera systems in churches has been precluded because of the expense. Dramatic changes have taken place, though, in the past few years.

Churches are now using closed-circuit television systems in a variety of ways:

- ❑ as a preview system before opening a locked door. By means of a camera mounted inside a glass door, a receptionist can see who is at a locked outer door before energizing an electric remote lock.
- ❑ as a hall monitor. Cameras placed in strategic hallways can allow a receptionist or other staff member to monitor who is in the building.
- ❑ as a room monitor. Many churches are using camera systems in nursery, preschool, and early education spaces,

both as a deterrent to potential child molestation and also as a liability protection for workers in these areas.

- ❑ as an exterior monitor. Cameras placed around the building's exterior tell would-be intruders that they are being watched.

Systems come in a variety of formats. Some issues you may want to consider are as follows:

- ❑ If the system calls for a single source and single monitor, such as a door monitor, then a simple one-unit camera hardwired to a monitor is all that is needed.
- ❑ Hardwired systems provide a more secure installation. When necessary, provide backup power to the system.
- ❑ If the use of the monitor system calls for a variety of spaces and cameras to be monitored, it would be more efficient to have one or two monitors that are fed camera input via a step-phase generator (for example, camera 1 is viewed for ten seconds, camera 2 for ten seconds, camera 3 for ten seconds, and so forth). Most security systems recommend that a space be viewed every minute. Using the step scheme above, you would need one monitor for every six cameras in use.
- ❑ If the area being monitored requires observation twenty-four hours a day, it would be appropriate to connect the camera to a video recorder that develops a twenty-four-hour tape. This type of system is used in banks, where a single frame is shot every five seconds. Slow-motion playback and stop-action pausing allow an observer to see who was in the space during the time loop.

One final word: Don't hide your camera systems. They serve as a deterrent. Let people know they are being watched. Place the cameras in a secure location but out in full view (for example, on the eaves of buildings, at doorways, in the corner of a room, and in Plexiglas domes in hallways and foyers.

## LOCK DOORS AND WINDOWS

It may seem too obvious to even mention the need to lock doors and windows, but law enforcement and insurance officials report that many instances of unwanted intrusion into church facilities occur through unlocked doors and windows. Unless you have some sort of expensive electronic lock-down system, this will be a problem that requires considerable effort to tackle. It is not so much a mechanical problem as it is a people problem.

People open doors; therefore it follows that people should shut and lock doors.

- ❑ Develop a policy stating that if an individual uses any type of key (mechanical or electronic) to open a door, he or she must immediately lock the door after entrance. Make this a part of the formal agreement when an individual is issued a key or is told a pass code.
- ❑ Designate who will open doors for events or church activities and who will make sure that the entrances are locked when the event is over. This will usually be a custodian or a staff member.
- ❑ An advantage of an electronic lock system is that the lock returns to the locked position after actuating, unless the individual knows the method for overriding the electronic bolt.

People open windows, therefore it follows that people should close and lock windows.

- ❑ Many regions of the country take advantage of spring and fall weather to let in fresh air from the outside. (Some areas are fortunate enough to be able to vent

---

Preschool and children areas require special thought when windows and doors are considered. Unless the room is also used by an academy or as a classroom or has items of particular value, it is suggested that the space have no lock—for two reasons: safety (a child needs to be able to move through the doorway in case of emergency) and security (a child could be locked in with no one else there to help him or her out, or an abuser could lock the door and molest a child). All doors to preschool and children areas should have window panes in the door. Many churches require this for any space that will contain individuals seventeen years of age or younger. If a privacy lock is placed in a toilet area, always make sure an emergency override key is located nearby.

Windows give a child a vista to God's world—but windows can also be a security hazard. Windows should be low enough for a child of the age group to look out. Use multiple-pane insulated or thermo-pane windows. Window frames should be metal or metal clad. Window opening and locking mechanisms should be "adult" high. On ground-floor windows and upper-floor windows in children's rooms, install heavy metal screens on the window. By affixing the screen with screws, the screen becomes a safety net for children who could tumble out, as well as a hindrance for an intruder trying to get in.

---

rooms even during the summer months.) A concerted effort must be made to train individuals who open the windows to close and lock them. Reminders in training literature, wall posters, notes, and church communication pieces will keep this need in front of them.

- ❑ Install window locks that take some effort to open. Some churches install keyed window locks; others use a pin that penetrates the sash and window frame.
- ❑ Mark locking devices so that the "open" position is quickly noticed. I asked my maintenance crew to paint the window locks with red paint so that the red portion of a locking system would be exposed to the room when the lock was opened. Someone in the room would then be able to see that the window was unlocked (I hope they'd notice an open window, too!), or the custodians, as they secured the building each evening, would pass by the room and detect a red, unlocked window.

## QUESTIONS FOR REFLECTION AND DISCUSSION

By now you may be in near panic, thinking that your church facility is the most unsecure space in the world. If this describes you, then one of this book's objectives has been met, namely, to make readers aware of security issues in the church facility.

Some of you may be thinking that you're not in such bad shape; you've got a problem here and there, but nothing a little time (and money) can't overcome. This is a good thing as well, because at least you now have a shopping list of what needs to be done.

Maybe a few of you are even wondering why you bought the book, because you have a fortress in which *everything* is safe and secure. For you I can only pray that your assessment is correct.

Let me go back to those of you who are wondering how in the world you'll ever provide a safe and secure church environment for every member of the church. Know this: you can't correct all your ills in one day. God himself took a half dozen days to create the world. There are some things you can do, however:

1. From the material discussed in chapters 3 and 4, what are some ways you can safeguard your church? Take a sheet or two of paper and create a list of practical security needs for your church.

2. Divide into three categories the items from the list of needs you've just created:

**Things You Can Do Immediately at No Cost**

**Things You Can Accomplish in the Near Future at Moderate Cost**

**Practical Security Needs That Require Planning and Budget Considerations**

3. Working with the organizational structure you created in chapter 2, how can you begin to address the items in the first category above? Be prepared to show some progress!

4. When appropriate, involve the entire church or parish in developing ways to solve security issues. Churches are in the people business. You may be surprised to see how many people in the church will share your motivation for a secure worship and learning environment.

**Paul E. Engle, Series Editor**

SERVING AS A CHURCH GREETER

This practical guidebook will help you reach out to people who need to experience the warmth of belonging to a church family. Includes tips for remembering names. **Softcover (ISBN 0-310-24764-0).**

SERVING AS A CHURCH USHER

Your impact as an usher is enormous both in meeting the needs of people and in keeping the church service running smoothly. **Softcover (ISBN 0-310-24763-2).**

SERVING IN YOUR CHURCH MUSIC MINISTRY

This wise, concise guidebook will help you harness your God-given musical talent as a gift to the body of Christ, in a way that brings joy to both God's heart and yours. Includes planning checklist. **Softcover (ISBN 0-310-24101-4).**

SERVING BY SAFEGUARDING YOUR CHURCH

Church ought to be the safest place on earth. Here's how to fulfill that goal in practical ways, Includes diagrams, checklists, and resources lists. **Softcover (ISBN 0-310-24105-7).**

SERVING IN CHURCH VISITATION

Whether visiting people in their homes, in the hospital, or in a restaurant over a cup of coffee, the simple act of connecting with others is filled with powerful possibilities. Includes do's and don'ts for various special-needs situations. **Softcover (ISBN 0-310-24103-0).**

***Pick up your copies today at your favorite bookstore!***

GRAND RAPIDS, MICHIGAN 49530 USA

WWW.ZONDERVAN.COM

We want to hear from you. Please send your comments about this book to us in care of the address below. Thank you.

GRAND RAPIDS, MICHIGAN 49530 USA
WWW.ZONDERVAN.COM